COUNTRY PROFILES

BOLIVIA

BY ALICIA Z. KLEPEIS

BELLWETHER MEDIA • MINNEAPOLIS, MN

This edition first published in 2023 by Bellwether Media, Inc.

No part of this publication may be reproduced in whole or in part without written permission of the publisher.
For information regarding permission, write to Bellwether Media, Inc., Attention: Permissions Department,
6012 Blue Circle Drive, Minnetonka, MN 55343.

Library of Congress Cataloging-in-Publication Data

Names: Klepeis, Alicia, 1971- author.
Title: Bolivia / by Alicia Z. Klepeis.
Description: Minneapolis, MN : Bellwether Media, 2023. | Series: [Country profiles] | Includes bibliographical references and index. | Audience: Ages 7-13 | Audience: Grades 4-6 | Summary: "Engaging images accompany information about Bolivia. The combination of high-interest subject matter and narrative text is intended for students in grades 3 through 8" Provided by publisher.
Identifiers: LCCN 2022050036 (print) | LCCN 2022050037 (ebook) | ISBN 9798886871463 (library binding) | ISBN 9798886872729 (ebook)
Subjects: LCSH: Bolivia–Juvenile literature.
Classification: LCC F3308.5 .K54 2023 (print) | LCC F3308.5 (ebook) | DDC 984–dc23/eng/20221021
LC record available at https://lccn.loc.gov/2022050036
LC ebook record available at https://lccn.loc.gov/2022050037

Text copyright © 2023 by Bellwether Media, Inc. BLASTOFF! DISCOVERY and associated logos are trademarks and/or registered trademarks of Bellwether Media, Inc.

Editor: Rachael Barnes   Designer: Brittany McIntosh

Printed in the United States of America, North Mankato, MN.

TABLE OF CONTENTS

MADIDI NATIONAL PARK	4
LOCATION	6
LANDSCAPE AND CLIMATE	8
WILDLIFE	10
PEOPLE	12
COMMUNITIES	14
CUSTOMS	16
SCHOOL AND WORK	18
PLAY	20
FOOD	22
CELEBRATIONS	24
TIMELINE	26
BOLIVIA FACTS	28
GLOSSARY	30
TO LEARN MORE	31
INDEX	32

MADIDI NATIONAL PARK

A family sleeps soundly inside their cabin in Madidi National Park. Soon, the squawks of macaws wake them up. They drink *api*, a hot drink made of corn, sugar, and cinnamon, before beginning their **rain forest** adventure. They head out onto a hiking trail to explore. An orange and black butterfly lands on a nearby branch.

BENI RIVER

OTHER TOP SITES

LAKE TITICACA

SALAR DE UYUNI

TIWANAKU

YUNGAS ROAD

   While the family enjoys a picnic lunch, a group of titi monkeys feast on fruits in the trees. Later that afternoon, the family takes a motorboat ride down the Beni River. They catch fish to cook for dinner. Welcome to Bolivia!

Bolivia is a nation in South America. Its area covers 424,164 square miles (1,098,581 square kilometers). The country has two capital cities. La Paz, in west-central Bolivia, is where the president and lawmakers work. Sucre is in south-central Bolivia. It is the **judicial** capital.

Bolivia is a **landlocked** country. Brazil wraps around the north and east. The Iténez River forms part of this long border. Paraguay stands to the southeast, and Argentina lies to the south. The Andes Mountains separate Bolivia from Chile in the southwest. Lake Titicaca makes up a section of the western border with Peru.

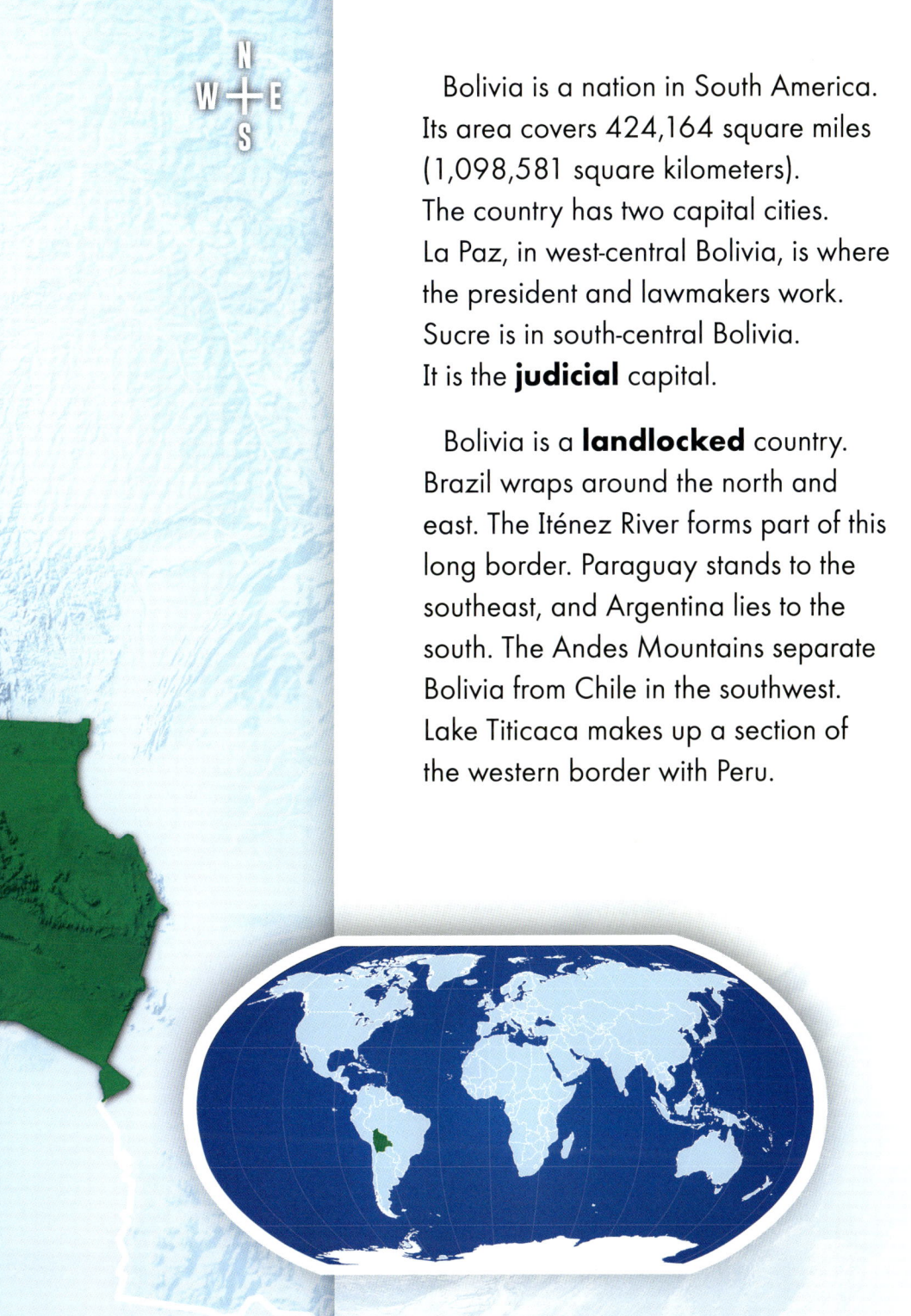

LANDSCAPE AND CLIMATE

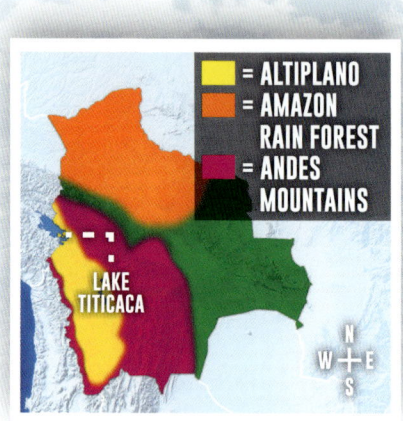

The high peaks of the Andes Mountains span part of western Bolivia. The mountains break into two ranges. In between is a **plateau** region called the *Altiplano*. It is home to Lake Titicaca. Northern Bolivia contains part of the Amazon Rain Forest. In the east is a large region called the Oriente. It has **tropical** lowlands, swamps, and grasslands. Southern Bolivia features valleys and hills.

STUNNING SALT FLATS

The world's biggest salt flat is *Salar de Uyuni*. It is located in the *Altiplano*. It was formed when ancient lakes dried up. Visitors can stay at a hotel made of salt!

ANDES MOUNTAINS

LA PAZ
Average seasonal highs and lows

JANUARY
HIGH: 59 °F (15 °C)
LOW: 40 °F (4 °C)

APRIL
HIGH: 60 °F (16 °C)
LOW: 34 °F (1 °C)

JULY
HIGH: 58 °F (14 °C)
LOW: 25 °F (-4 °C)

OCTOBER
HIGH: 62 °F (17 °C)
LOW: 35 °F (2 °C)

°F = degrees Fahrenheit
°C = degrees Celsius

Much of Bolivia has a **humid** climate. Fog often fills the rain forest. The highlands are cooler than the lower areas. The country has a rainy season from December to March.

WILDLIFE

In the highlands of Bolivia, vicuñas and guanacos **graze** on grasses and shrubs. Giant Andean condors fly above. They search for **carrion** to eat. Flocks of flamingos gather on the shores of Lakes Titicaca and Poopó. They **migrate** to different areas throughout the year.

Giant otters splash and swim in Bolivia's tropical rain forest rivers. They feed on fish. The feathers of royal flycatchers and blue-backed manakins are pops of color among the trees. Marsh deer run from pumas on open lowlands.

GIANT OTTER

PUMA

CAPYBARAS

ANDEAN CONDOR

COOL CAPYBARAS

Weighing up to 174 pounds (79 kilograms), capybaras are the biggest rodents in the world. They live in the lowland areas east of the Andes Mountains. They spend a lot of time in water. They even sleep in rivers!

VICUÑA

VICUÑA

Life Span: 15 to 20 years
Red List Status: least concern

vicuña range =

| LEAST CONCERN | NEAR THREATENED | VULNERABLE | ENDANGERED | CRITICALLY ENDANGERED | EXTINCT IN THE WILD | EXTINCT |

PEOPLE

Over 12 million people live in Bolivia. More than 2 out of 3 are *mestizos*. They have both **Indigenous** and European **ancestors**. There are also many Indigenous people in Bolivia. The Aymara and Quechua are the largest groups. Smaller groups of people in Bolivia have European and African ancestors.

Most Bolivians are Christian. About 7 out of 10 people are Roman Catholic. Many Bolivians are **bilingual**. More people speak Spanish than any other language in Bolivia. But Spanish is just one of 37 official languages. The others are languages of Indigenous people.

FAMOUS FACE
Name: Luzmila Carpio
Birthday: 1949
Hometown: Qala Qala, Bolivia
Famous for: A singer who has helped bring the music of Bolivia's Quechua people to the world

SPEAK SPANISH

ENGLISH	SPANISH	HOW TO SAY IT
hello	hola	OH-la
goodbye	adiós	ah-dee-OHS
please	por favor	pohr fah-VOR
thank you	gracias	grah-SEE-ahs
yes	sí	SEE
no	no	noh

SUCRE

COMMUNITIES

TONS OF TREES

Mi Arbol is a tree-planting program in Bolivia. The government is spending money to replant trees where they were cut down in the past. The goal is to plant 6 million trees across the country.

LA PAZ

About 7 out of 10 Bolivians live in **urban** areas. The country's largest city, La Paz, is home to nearly 2 million people. Most people in city centers live in apartments. Stand-alone homes are common in the surrounding areas. People typically travel by bus or taxi. Locals also use the cable car system in La Paz.

Country homes are often built of **adobe** bricks with straw or wooden roofs. Cement walls and iron roofs are becoming more popular. **Rural** Bolivians often ride bikes to get around. Many families struggle to have enough food to eat. But most people have access to clean water.

CUSTOMS

Bolivia has a rich **tradition** of folk arts. Artists have created beautiful **textiles**, like woven blankets, for thousands of years. Wood carvings and masks are also popular art forms. Bolivian music is celebrated around the world. The panpipe is a well-known instrument from the Andes region. The *charango*, a stringed instrument, is traditionally made of an armadillo shell!

BOATS AND BASKETS

People in the Lake Titicaca area make many objects from locally grown totora reeds. Some create beautiful baskets. Others build lightweight boats. They even make islands from these plants where people can live!

Most Bolivians wear modern clothes. But Indigenous people in rural areas commonly wear traditional clothing. Some women may wear colorful skirts called *polleras*. Many wear bowler hats and shawls, too. Men may wear shin-length pants with a shirt and leather belt.

SCHOOL AND WORK

PRIMARY SCHOOL STUDENTS IN SANTA CRUZ

Children in Bolivia begin school at age 6. Primary school lasts for eight years. Most schools have a morning shift and an afternoon shift. Some students need to work for half the day to help their families. Classes are mostly taught in Spanish. But schools are expected to teach Indigenous languages, too. Children are not required to complete high school.

Nearly half of the Bolivian population have **service jobs**. Some have jobs in transportation or communications. Others work in hotels or as guides for **tourists**. Bolivian workers **mine** for gold and tin. Farmers grow sugarcane, soybeans, and grains.

TOUR GUIDE

LOTS OF LITHIUM

Bolivia's salt flats hold more than half of the lithium found on Earth. This mineral is used in batteries for electronic devices. Cell phones and electric cars both need it.

PROCESSING LITHIUM

PLAY

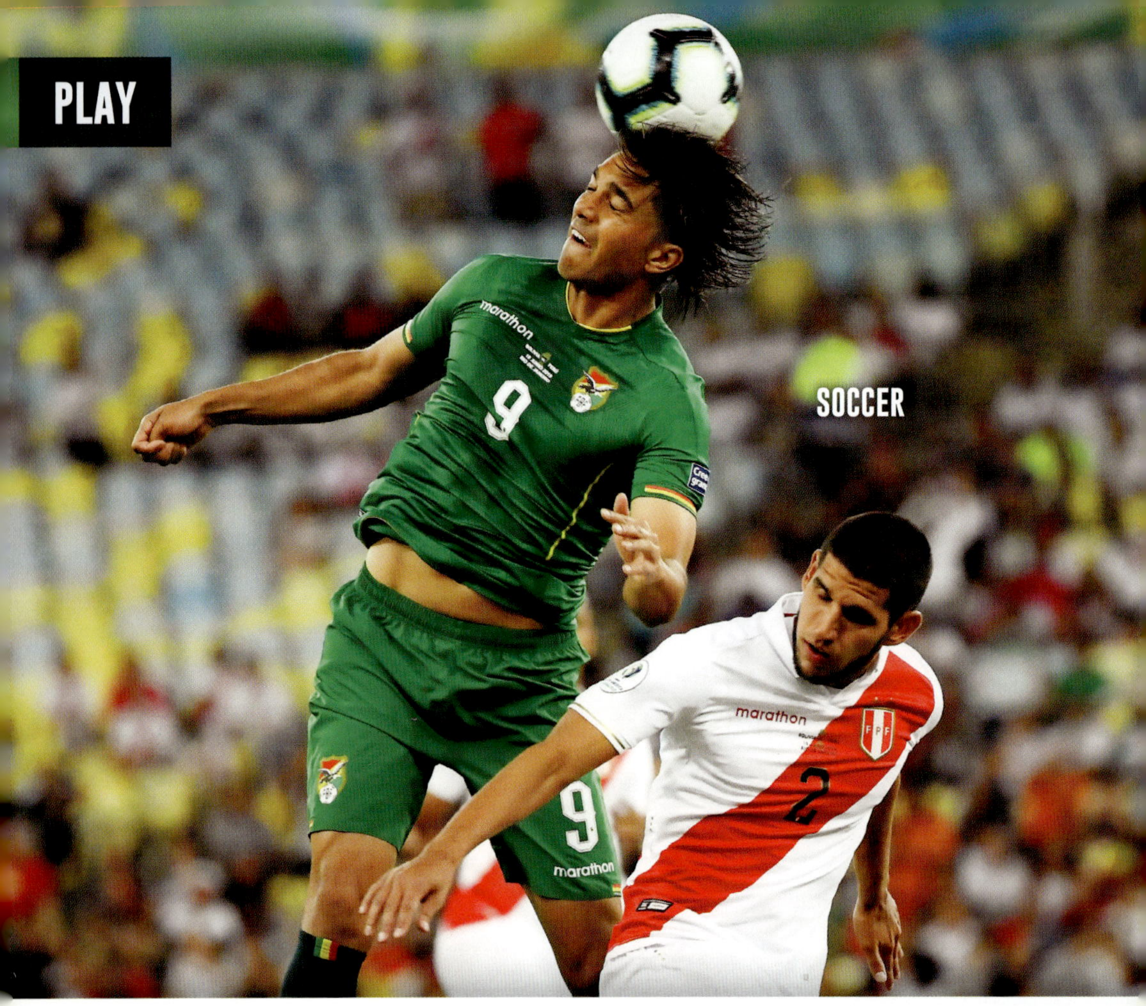

SOCCER

Bolivians young and old are huge soccer fans. People play and watch all over the country. Volleyball and basketball are also popular sports. Some Bolivians take part in horseback riding, tennis, and golf. Families in cities often visit parks and playgrounds in their free time.

HORSEBACK RIDING

People in Bolivia spend time with friends and family both in homes and in town **plazas**. Dancing is another popular pastime throughout the nation. Urban dwellers also enjoy going to movie theaters. They often play games or chat online at internet cafes.

PLAZA

MAKE A SPINNING TOP

Many children in Bolivia play games with spinning wooden tops. Some do tricks. Others just spin to see whose stays upright the longest. Create your top from materials in your home!

What You Need:
- a round plastic lid
- a permanent marker
- a ruler
- a nail
- colorful decorations like beads or sequins
- glue
- a bamboo skewer
- scissors

What You Do:
1. Find a small round plastic lid, about 3 inches (7.6 centimeters) wide.
2. Measure across the top of the lid. Use your marker to draw a dot in the center of the lid.
3. Have an adult help you make a small hole in the lid. Use the nail to poke through the dot you drew.
4. Avoiding the hole in the lid, glue some decorations on the top of the lid. Let it dry thoroughly.
5. Place the bamboo skewer through the hole in your lid. The sharp end should be at the bottom. If the skewer is too long, you can trim it at the top with your scissors.
6. Use your hands to spin the skewer. How long did it stay in motion? Get a friend to make a top, too. Compete to see whose top spins the longest.

FOOD

A FANTASTIC FRUIT
Banana passionfruit is a favorite fruit in Bolivia. Its oval shape and yellowish skin make it look similar to a banana. But inside, its juicy pulp is sweet and tastes like an orange.

PREPARING SOPA DE MANI

A common breakfast or morning snack in Bolivia is *salteñas*. These baked pastries are typically filled with meat and a flavorful sauce. Cooks throughout the nation often serve soups and stews, especially as part of lunch. *Fricasé* is a thick, spicy soup containing chicken or pork. Potatoes and pasta thicken a popular peanut soup called *sopa de mani*.

Majadito is well-loved in the tropical lowlands. Spicy rice is served with beef jerky, vegetables, fried bananas, and a fried egg. *Sajta de pollo* is a popular boiled chicken dish from western Bolivia. It is often served with freeze-dried potatoes called *chuños*.

SALTEÑAS

MAJADITO

COCADAS (COCONUT COOKIES)

Make this tasty treat for a dessert or afternoon tea. It is quite sweet. Have an adult help you prepare it.

Ingredients:
2 2/3 cups unsweetened dried coconut
3/4 cup condensed milk
1 egg, lightly beaten
1/4 teaspoon vanilla or almond extract
pinch of salt
parchment paper, butter, or cooking spray for the pan

Steps:
1. Place all of the ingredients into a large bowl. Mix until well combined. Let this mixture sit for 10 minutes.
2. Cover a baking sheet with parchment paper or coat it with butter or cooking spray.
3. Use your hands or an ice cream scoop to form roughly 24 balls.
4. Bake at 325 degrees Fahrenheit (163 degrees Celsius) for 20 to 25 minutes, or until light brown.
5. Let cool on the baking sheet for a few minutes. Enjoy!

CELEBRATIONS

CARNAVAL IN ORURO

Each February or March before Lent, Bolivians across the country host festive events for *Carnaval*. Incredible parades featuring costumed dancers are part of the fun. The Carnaval celebrations in Oruro are the most famous in Bolivia. Many Christians also celebrate **Holy Week** by attending church.

Every year, Bolivians recognize their independence from Spain on August 6. School children often take part in parades to celebrate. People have feasts on All Saints' Day in November. They also honor loved ones by visiting and placing flowers on their graves. Bolivians are proud of their **culture** all year long!

DAY OF THE SEA

On March 23, Bolivians remember when the country lost their border along the sea in the War of the Pacific. Bands play music, and Bolivian navy sailors take part in the celebrations.

SUCRE

TIMELINE

1824
Simón Bolívar, a freedom fighter from Venezuela, frees Bolivia from Spanish rule

AROUND 500-900 CE
The Tiwanaku Empire, including its capital near Lake Titicaca, is well-established

1836
Bolivia joins a federation with Peru, which ends three years later

1825
Bolivia becomes an independent nation

1538
All of present-day Bolivia falls under Spain's control

1884
Bolivia loses its access to the ocean, following the War of the Pacific with Chile

1990
Four million acres of rain forest are given to Bolivia's Indigenous people

2010
Peru gives Bolivia permission to build a Pacific port on its land

2006
Evo Morales, Bolivia's first Indigenous president, takes office

2014
The Andean Road System, which runs through Bolivia and five other South American countries, becomes a UNESCO World Heritage Site

BOLIVIA FACTS

Official Name: Plurinational State of Bolivia

Flag of Bolivia: Three horizontal stripes make up the flag of Bolivia. The top one is red and represents bravery. The middle stripe is yellow and stands for the country's mineral resources. The bottom one is green. It is a symbol of the country's rich lands. When flown by the government, the flag's yellow stripe holds Bolivia's coat of arms. Since 2009, the Bolivian flag must be flown along with a Wiphala. This square flag is multicolored. It stands for the nation's Indigenous people.

Area: 424,164 square miles (1,098,581 square kilometers)

Capital Cities: La Paz, Sucre

Important Cities: Santa Cruz, Cochabamba

Population: 12,054,379 (2022 est.)

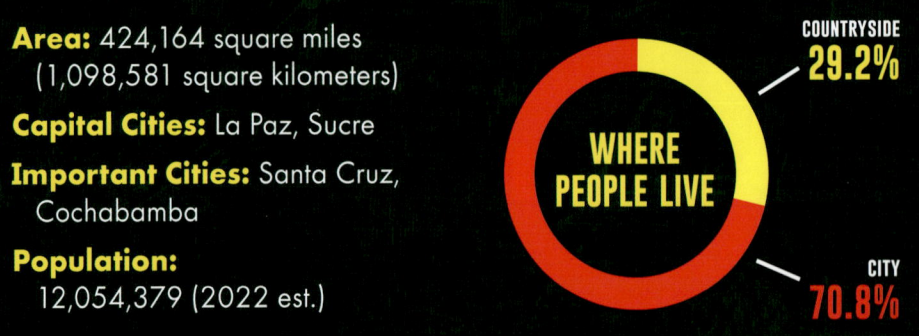

WHERE PEOPLE LIVE
COUNTRYSIDE 29.2%
CITY 70.8%

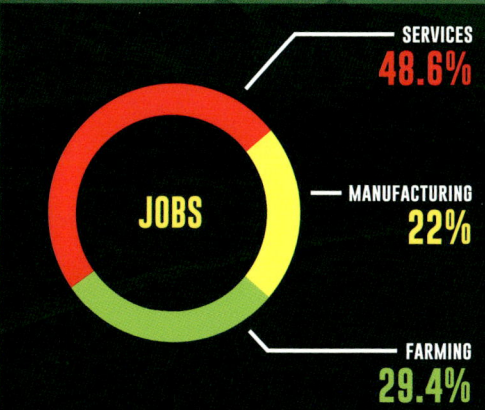

Main Exports:

natural gas

gold

zinc and other metal ores

soybean products

National Holiday:
Independence Day, August 6

Main Languages:
Spanish and 33 Indigenous languages including Quechua, Aymara, and Guarani (official)

Form of Government:
presidential republic

Title for Country Leader:
president (head of government and chief of state)

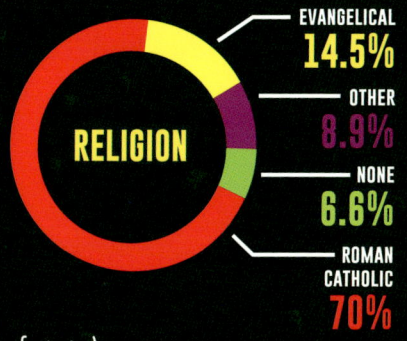

Unit of Money:
Bolivian boliviano

GLOSSARY

adobe—bricks made of clay and straw that are dried in the sun

ancestors—relatives who lived long ago

bilingual—able to speak two languages

carrion—the meat of dead animals

culture—the beliefs, arts, and ways of life in a place or society

graze—to eat grass or other plants that are growing in a field or pasture

Holy Week—the week before Easter

humid—having a lot of moisture in the air

Indigenous—related to people originally from an area

judicial—related to the court system of a country

landlocked—completely surrounded by land

migrate—to travel from one place to another, often with the seasons

mine—to dig under the ground for materials, such as minerals, coal, or gas

plateau—an area of flat, raised land

plazas—public squares in cities or towns

rain forest—a thick, green forest that receives a lot of rain

rural—related to the countryside

service jobs—jobs that perform tasks for people or businesses

textiles—fabrics that are woven or knit

tourists—people who travel to visit another place

tradition—a custom, idea, or belief handed down from one generation to the next

tropical—part of the tropics; the tropics is a hot, rainy region near the equator.

urban—related to cities and city life

TO LEARN MORE

AT THE LIBRARY

Goldish, Meish. *Bolivia*. New York, N.Y.: Bearport Publishing, 2020.

Lassieur, Allison. *Inca Civilization*. Lake Elmo, Minn.: Focus Readers, 2020.

Rohan, Rebecca Carey. *Bolivia*. New York, N.Y.: Cavendish Square Publishing, 2022.

ON THE WEB

FACTSURFER

Factsurfer.com gives you a safe, fun way to find more information.

1. Go to www.factsurfer.com.
2. Enter "Bolivia" into the search box and click 🔍.
3. Select your book cover to see a list of related content.

INDEX

activities, 4, 5, 20, 21
All Saints' Day, 25
Amazon Rain Forest, 4, 8, 9, 10
Andes Mountains, 7, 8, 9, 10, 16
arts, 16
capital (see La Paz and Sucre)
Carnaval, 24
Carpio, Luzmila, 13
celebrations, 24–25
climate, 9
communities, 14–15
customs, 16–17
Day of the Sea, 25
education, 18
fast facts, 28–29
food, 4, 5, 15, 22–23, 25
Holy Week, 24
housing, 14, 15
Independence Day, 25

La Paz, 6, 7, 9, 14
Lake Titicaca, 7, 8, 10, 16
landmarks, 4, 5, 8
landscape, 4, 5, 7, 8–9, 10, 16, 19, 23
language, 13, 18
location, 6–7
Madidi National Park, 4–5
music, 16, 25
people, 12–13, 17
recipe, 23
religion, 13, 24
size, 7
spinning top (activity), 21
sports, 20
Sucre, 6, 7, 13, 25
timeline, 26–27
transportation, 14, 15, 19
wildlife, 4, 5, 10–11
work, 18, 19

The images in this book are reproduced through the courtesy of: SL-Photography, front cover, p. 21; Elzbieta Sekowska, pp. 4-5; flocu, p. 5 (Lake Titicaca); blubery, p. 5 (Salar de Uyuni); Cezary Wojtkowski, p. 5 (Tiwanaku); StreetFlash, p. 5 (Yungas Road); Stefano Paterna/ Alamy, p. 8; Alan_Tow, p. 9 (Andes Mountains); Jc valenzuela, p. 9 (La Paz); BearFotos, p. 10 (Andean condor); OSTILL is Franck Camhi, p. 10 (giant otter); Holly Kuchera, p. 10 (puma); buteo, p. 10 (capybaras); Wirestock Creators, p. 11 (vicuña); Jam Travels, p. 12; ANNE-CHRISTINE POUJOULAT/ Getty Images, p. 13 (Luzmila Carpio); saiko3p, p. 13 (Sucre); Renata Tizzo, p. 14; Matyas Rehak/ Alamy, p. 15; Steve Allen Travel Photography/ Alamy, p. 16; NICOLA MESSANA PHOTOS, p. 17; Sjors737, p. 18; David Vilaplana/ Alamy, pp. 19 (tour guide), 20 (horseback riding); Gaston Brito Miserocchi / Stringer/ Getty Images, p. 19 (processing lithium); A.PAES, p. 20 (soccer); Alexandre Laprise, p. 22 (preparing sopa de mani); Olga Popova, p. 22 (banana passionfruit); Ildi Papp, p. 23 (salteñas); Fanfo, p. 23 (majadito); Milton Buzon, p. 23 (cocadas); Curioso.Photography, p. 24; sduraku, p. 25; Frederic Legrand - COMEO, p. 27 (Evo Morales); Carlos Sala Fotografia, p. 27 (Pacific port); Ivan Vdovin/ Alamy, p. 29 (boliviano).